SPOT IT!
LIMIT
25
AIRPORT TOWING
Safety and Service
HIGHWAY PATROL
USA
RESCUE
77
STOP
U.S. COAST GUARD
SCHOOL BUS
STOP
6947
SAFARI
F.D.N.
AMBULANCE
WRONG
WAY
CEMENT

DO NOT ENTER
YIELD
SPEED LIMIT 25
AIRPORT TOWING
UNITED
HIGHWAY PATROL
Safety and Service
TEXACO FIRE CHIEF
POLICE
AMBULANCE
CEMENT
9852

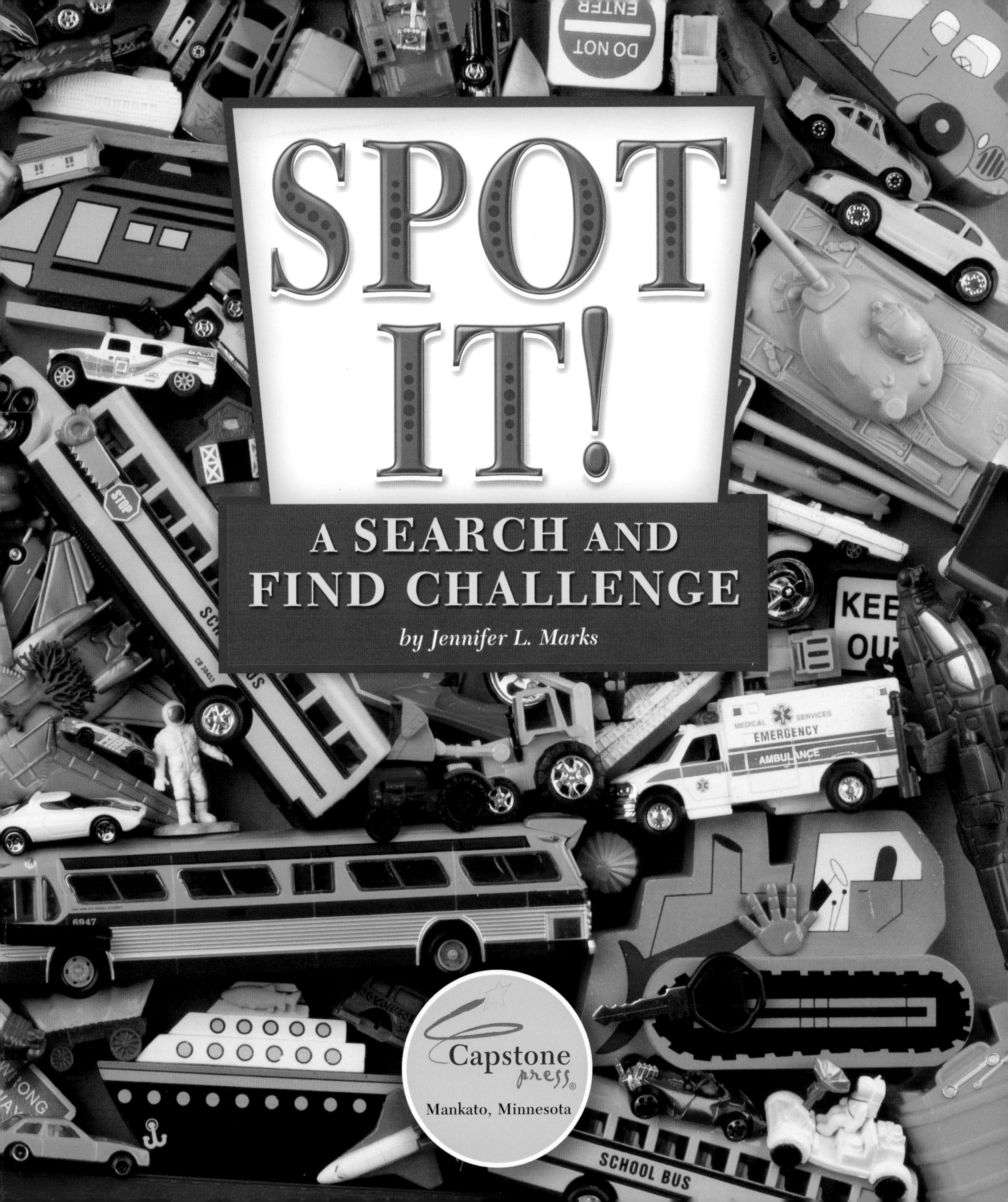

SPOT IT!
A SEARCH AND FIND CHALLENGE
by Jennifer L. Marks
Capstone press
Mankato, Minnesota
DO NOT ENTER
STOP
MEDICAL SERVICES
EMERGENCY
AMBULANCE
SCHOOL BUS
6947

Published by Capstone Press,
151 Good Counsel Drive, P.O. Box 669, Mankato, Minnesota 56002.
www.capstonepress.com

Printed in the United States of America, North Mankato, Minnesota.

042010
005684R

Library of Congress Cataloging-in-Publication Data
Marks, Jennifer, 1979–
Spot It!: A Search and Find Challenge / by Jennifer L. Marks.
p. cm.
Includes bibliographical references.
ISBN 978-1-4296-4252-1 (library binding)
1. Picture puzzles — Juvenile literature. I. Title.
GV1507.P47M274 2010
793.73 — dc22 2009026887

Credits

Ted Williams, book designer
Juliette Peters, set designer
Len Epstein, illustrator
All photos by Capstone Press Photo Studio

The author dedicates this book to Roger and Sandy Wittrock of Savage, Minnesota.

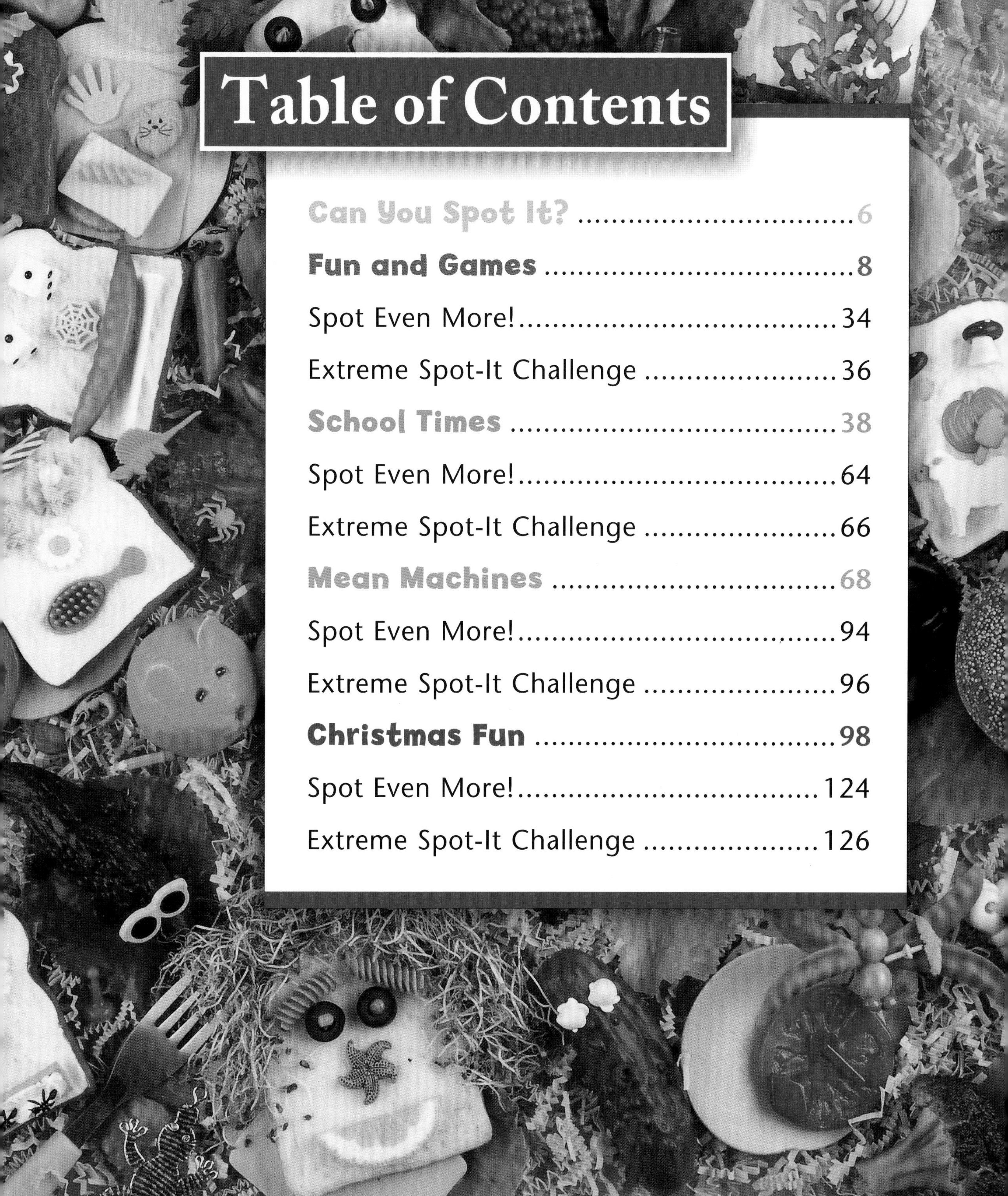

Table of Contents

You'll have a ball!
It's a piece of cake!
What luck! A clover!
Bb
C
Dd
STOP
Jj
TEAM
Tt
consonants:
b c d f g h
l m n p q r

Can You Spot It?

Think you have eagle eyes? Can't get enough seek-and-find fun? Challenge yourself with this amazing collection of Spot-It puzzles and search for hours!

Discover dazzling holiday scenes, creepy cafeteria meals, wacky outdoor sports, crazy construction zones, and more. Every photograph is packed with hidden objects. Every clue leads you on a new search.

To truly test your seeking skills, check out the Spot Even More! clues and the Extreme Spot-It Challenge puzzles at the end of each chapter.

ALIEN
AIRPORT TOWING
FIRE BRIGADE

FUN and GAMES

Tickets
TICKET
713225
KEEP THIS COUPON
TICKET
KEEP THIS COUPON
Miracle Bubbles
CLASSIC
1 3 5 7
9 11 13 15
2 4 6 8
10 12 14

Step Right Up

Can you spot . . .

- a blue bunny?
- four bowling pins?
- a yo-yo?
- a puppy?
- a helicopter?
- a handkerchief?

Does This Bug You?

Can you spot . . .

- a football?
- two happy flowers?
- a garden tool?
- a fish?
- three red mushrooms?
- a treasure chest?

Just Playin'

Can you spot . . .

- two baseball bats?
- a pineapple?
- a first prize?
- a red balloon?
- a taxicab?
- a police car?

ONE WAY

PASSPORT

Let's Pretend

Can you spot . . .

- a whistle?
- a sea horse?
- an apple?
- two hearts?
- a red boat?
- a green feather?

Vid Kid
Can you spot . . .
a bike?
an ice cream cone?
a baseball glove?
two apple cores?
a blue "X"?
an upside-down tree?
Nintendo
"SLURP"
Reject
PIZZA
KEEP OUT!
NYKO

TIME
1:38
SCORE
5,738
Hey Looky Me!
SNIFF
SNIFF
LOSERS
YUM!
GULP!
MakeUp
CANDY
SPORTS
TRASH MONSTER #1
"DO NOT OPEN!"
Dear John
MILK
NOTE Book

Hocus Pocus

Can you spot . . .

- a flying bird?
- a fire truck?
- a tiny wizard?
- a pen?
- a star shadow?
- a red mitten?

Life's a Beach

Can you spot . . .

- two scuba divers?
- a pink butterfly?
- a red flag?
- a panda's face?
- two fire hydrants?
- four yellow buttons?

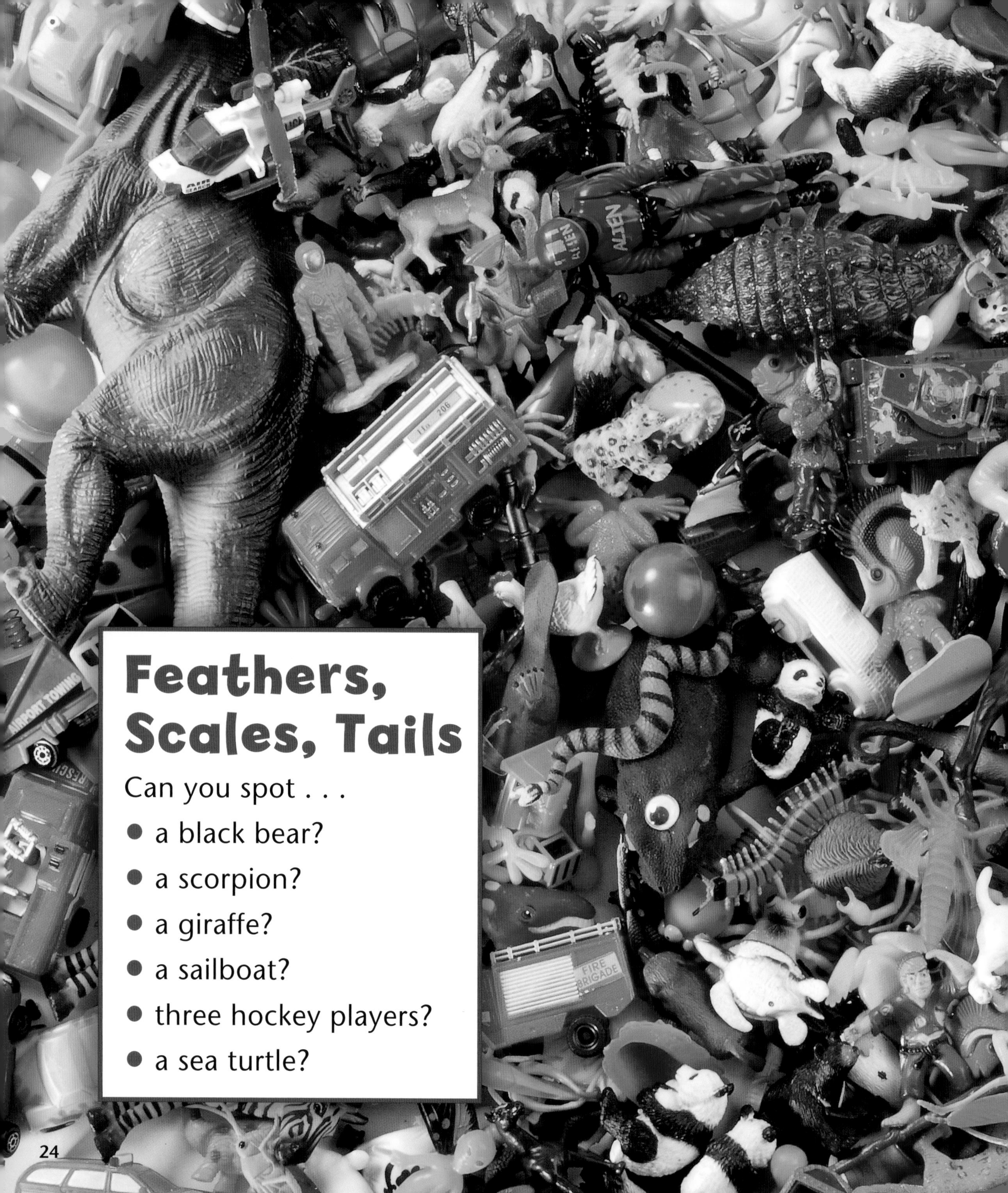

Feathers, Scales, Tails

Can you spot . . .

- a black bear?
- a scorpion?
- a giraffe?
- a sailboat?
- three hockey players?
- a sea turtle?

TURBO
959
SAFARI

You are invited!

Who Needs Sleep?

Can you spot . . .

- a flamingo?
- a tack?
- two sets of keys?
- two sheep?
- two golf tees?
- a sleepy kitty?

Boys of Summer

Can you spot . . .

- a cardinal?
- two yellow hands?
- a catcher?
- two paper clips?
- a baby seal?
- a leaf of lettuce?

#1
FAN
FLORIDA
MARLINS
GIANTS
Mets
CHICAGO
CUBS
B
Braves
TICKET
713246
KEEP THIS
COUPON

Play with Your Food

Can you spot . . .

- a shamrock?
- a crown?
- a roller skate?
- a tractor?
- a turtle?
- a green sled?

On the Lawn

Can you spot . . .

- two poodles?
- a plane?
- a marble?
- two gnomes?
- a dog bone?
- a sunflower?

HOME RUN 100
TRIPLE 75
DOUBLE 50
Rawlings
GOLF
YOXO!

Spot Even More!

10 Step Right Up

Look for a gray elephant face, a yellow bow, a clown juggling, a pink paper clip, and chattering teeth.

12 Does This Bug You?

See if you can spot a rabbit, a pinecone, a chair, three scorpions, a baboon, a pink tulip, and a stingray.

14 Just Playin'

Take another look to find an anchor, an orange button, a ghost, a bunch of grapes, and an ice cream bar.

16 Let's Pretend

Now find a fork, a pink comb, a jumbo diamond, a bobber, a sword, and a big pair of lips.

18 Vid Kid

Now spot a seagull, a stick of dynamite, two boots, cracked eyeglasses, money, and a milk carton.

20 Hocus Pocus

This time find a red bear, a lion, a pineapple, a scissors, a blue bear, a cherry, and the letter Y.

22 Life's a Beach

See if you can find a wind surfer, two white daisies, a pinwheel, a sand castle, and a gold necklace.

24 Feathers, Scales, Tails

Try to find a safari jeep, a black bat, a spinning top, a koala, a chicken, and a googly eye.

26 Who Needs Sleep?

Now spot a mouse, two ballet slippers, a wrench, a spatula, a dove, an orange shirt, and an apple.

28 Boys of Summer

Try to find a dalmatian, a blue car, a carrot, a cowboy hat, a bunch of bananas, and a moon.

30 Play with Your Food

Now look for an arrow, a slice of cake, a number 3, a cactus, a spiderweb, and three pieces of broccoli.

32 On the Lawn

Try to spot an astronaut, two millipedes, a walrus, a button, a turtle, and a blue jack.

Extreme Spot-It Challenge

Just can't get enough Spot-It action? Here's an extra fun-and-games challenge. Try to spot:

- **two parrots**
- **the letter H**
- **a yellow airplane**
- **two sea stars**
- **a ghost**
- **a black housefly**
- **the letter Y**
- **a skunk**
- **a mermaid**
- **a grasshopper**
- **a pair of eyeglasses**
- **a cherry**
- **a monkey wearing a hat**
- **an orange airplane**
- **two plastic turtles**
- **a scuba diver**
- **two orange cones**

consonants:
b c d f g h
j k l m n p q r

SCHOOL TIMES

11
Good for You!
black
ENGINE CO.
NO. 9
50 120
40 100
30 80

First Stop: My Locker

Can you spot . . .

- a tortoise?
- a lizard?
- a trophy?
- a comb?
- a bowling pin?
- a green car?

Best Teacher!
R
SCHOOL BUS
FIRST AID
GLUE
1st
Boys' Hall Pass
Dinosaur
Dinosaurio
BEST TEACHER
September
TUESDAY
WEDNESDAY
FRIDAY
STOP
NO STANDING
I LOVE TO READ

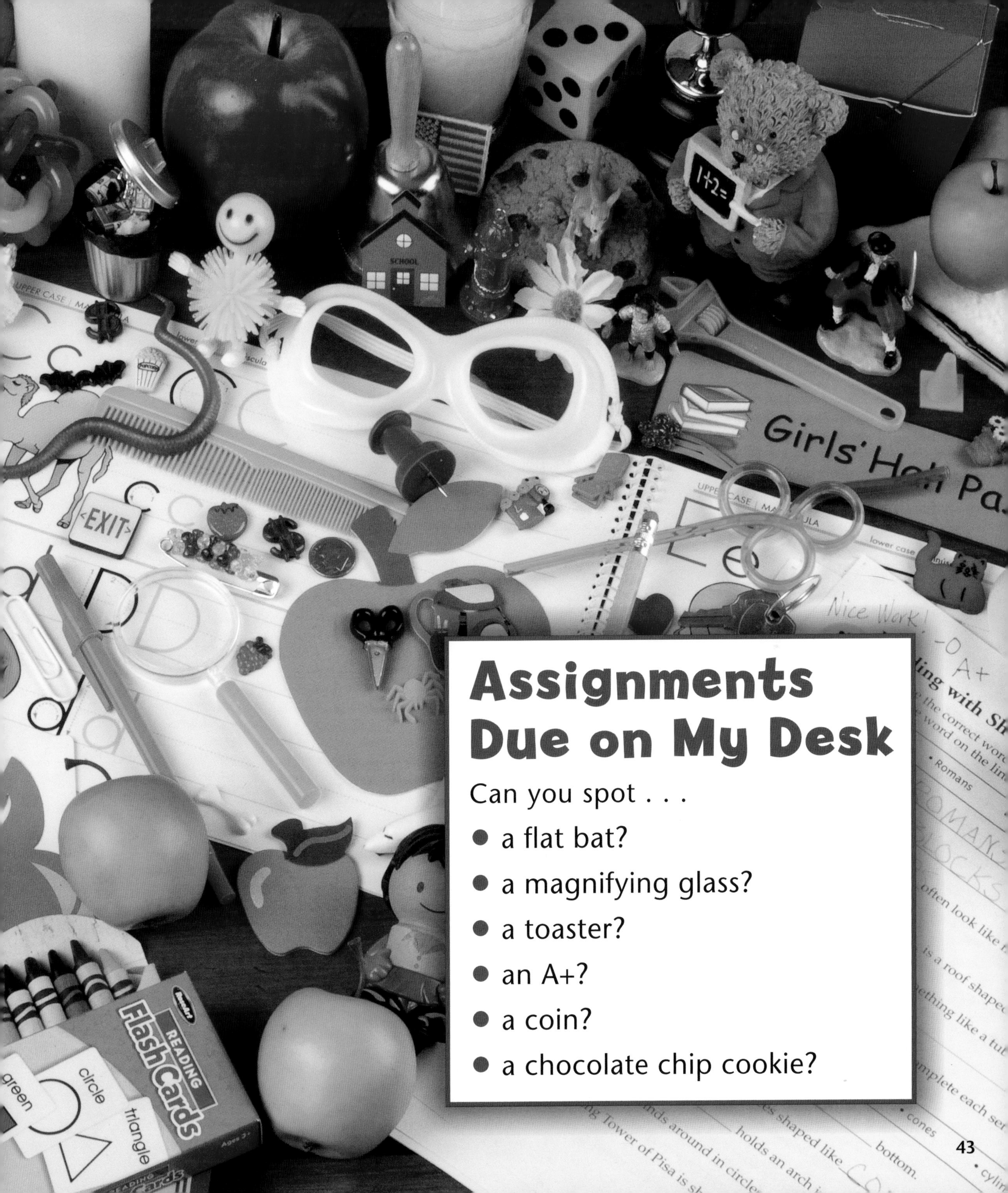

Assignments Due on My Desk

Can you spot . . .

- a flat bat?
- a magnifying glass?
- a toaster?
- an A+?
- a coin?
- a chocolate chip cookie?

consonants:
b c d f g h
k l m n p q r
STOP
TEAM
Tt
Dd
Bb
YoYo

"P" Is for Pickle

Can you spot . . .

- a tennis racket?
- a giraffe?
- a trophy?
- a pickle?
- a slice of pizza?
- a rainbow?

Dictionary
The Solar Syste
Science
Bugs, Bugs,
Trees and Honey

Weird Science

Can you spot . . .

- a rat?
- a mustache?
- five frogs?
- a windmill?
- a clover?
- a snake?

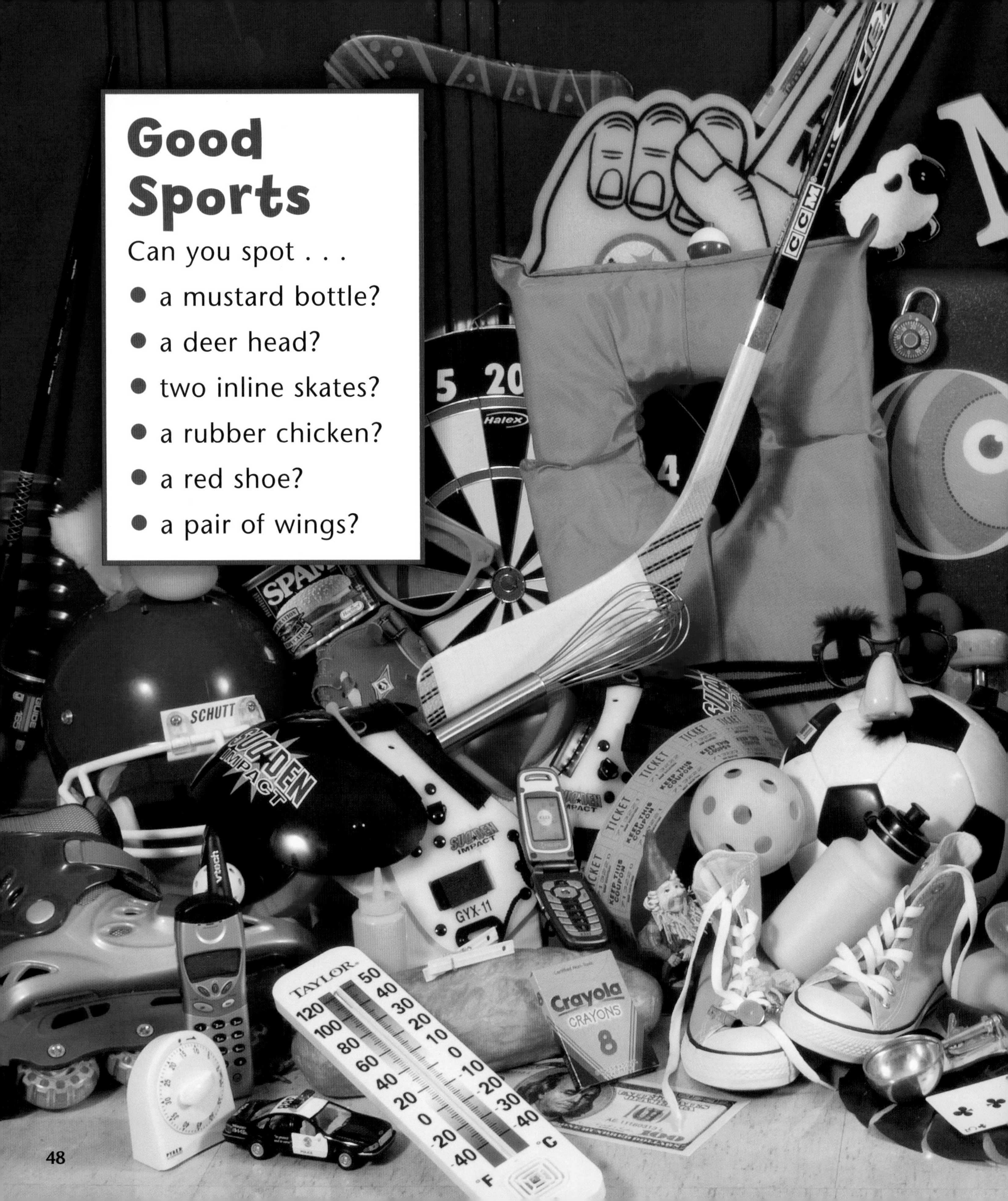

Good Sports

Can you spot . . .

- a mustard bottle?
- a deer head?
- two inline skates?
- a rubber chicken?
- a red shoe?
- a pair of wings?

8
Wilson
SELL BY
2% Reduced Fat Milk
Wilson
2
Wilson
GRAND
SPORT DESIGN
POPCORN
7

Sally,
Don't forget to
eat your apple
Love
2% Reduced
YIELD
yellow
SCHOOL BUS
Well Done!

You Gonna Eat That?

Can you spot . . .

- a tiny teddy bear?
- four croutons?
- a silver whistle?
- two ice cubes?
- a cowboy boot?
- a balloon?

Recess, at Last!

Can you spot . . .

- a dragon?
- a hammer?
- an ear of corn?
- a football?
- a yellow button?
- a saddle?

SCHOOL BUS
985

FOOD CHAIN
ASSIGNMENT "IN BOX"
ADVANCED ASTROPHYSICS
Tissues
Weird Comics
TRASH

A Whiteboard Class-tastrophy

Can you spot . . .

- a jump rope?
- a big sneeze?
- eight sheep?
- two fish?
- a dribble of drool?
- a shepherd's cane?

We Heart Art

Can you spot . . .

- a paper chain?
- a brown nest with eggs?
- a box of floss?
- a xylophone?
- a tiny panda?
- a unicorn?

ONE WAY
A B C
Notes
GLUE
22
CHINESE CHECKERS
BROWN
tub
GOOD WORK

The Star Spangled Banner
120
100
80
60
40
20
0
-20
-40
°F

And the Band Marches On

Can you spot . . .

- chatty teeth?
- a triangle?
- a slinky?
- a spotted flip-flop?
- a bunny?
- a sheriff's badge?

Totally Busted!

Can you spot . . .

- an astronaut?
- two wads of gum?
- a cotton swab?
- barbecue sauce?
- a nail clipper?
- a little dog?

TWENTY DOLLARS
A+ worker!
B·B·Q
HEARTY ORIGINAL
BICYCLE
RIDER
MILK BONE
MARINA
30 86
29 84
28 82
27 80
26 78
24 76
23 74
22 72
°C °F
USA First-Class
NORTH CAROLINA
Glue Stick
A B C

The Dog Ate My Homework

Can you spot . . .

- a hot dog?
- a toothpick?
- a fuzzy duck?
- a sandwich?
- two combs?
- a bottle of glue?

1st PLACE
+2
rug
car
cat
bat
mat
sat
rat
pat
rug
mug
bug
dug
hug
jug

Spot Even More!

40 First Stop: My Locker

See if you can spot a pink letter X, a blue snake, a carrot, a green lock, a paper crane, and a dragonfly.

42 Assignments Due on My Desk

Try to find a ruler, a space shuttle, a cowbell, a mouse, and a banana.

44 "P" Is for Pickle

Take another look and find a horseshoe, a blue eyeball, keys, a moose, a red shoe, and a blue house.

46 Weird Science

Now find a box of popcorn, two white daisies, an ant, a pretzel, a tiny bone, and a gummy worm.

48 Good Sports

Now spot a $100 bill, two water bottles, three Wiffle balls, two goggles, a gnome, and a blue car.

50 You Gonna Eat That?

Take another look and find a football helmet, a bunch of matches, a cockroach, and a construction cone.

52 Recess, at Last!

See if you can find a golden crown, a scissors, a red sweatband, an alley cat, and purple sandals.

54 A Whiteboard Class-tastrophy

Now spot a nose-picker, a bag of frogs, a mailbox, and a mouse hole.

56 We Heart Art

Try to find a beehive, a blue ribbon, a blue button, a pumpkin, a pea pod, and a school bus.

58 And the Band Marches On

Try to find a blue head, two pink shoes, a feather duster, and an army tank.

60 Totally Busted!

Now look for a blue shark, a battleship, a deck of cards, a toothbrush, and a tiny yellow pencil.

62 The Dog Ate My Homework

Try to spy a hiker, a spoon, a parrot, a bandage, a clothespin, and a snake.

SCHOOL
Ff
Dd
GLUE
SCHOOL BUS
SCHOOL
USA
POLICE
Bee Happy
1+1=2
A B C
MILK
PAINT
BANDAGES

Extreme Spot-It Challenge

Just can't get enough Spot-It action? Try this extra credit challenge. See if you can spot:

- a bottle of glue
- a strand of pearls
- a three-leafed clover
- seven daisies
- five baseballs
- three zebras
- a yellow car
- a red pen
- two school buses
- a teddy bear
- two bunches of grapes
- two bunnies
- an orange fish
- a pinwheel
- three smiling skulls
- a bunch of carrots
- a spelling test

3
United States
USA
FIRST
AID
ONE WAY

MEAN MACHINES

BUGLES
44
3
48
SIGNATURE
E-040
METRO EMERGENCY
Valvoline
Ultimate
AMOCO
Kellogg's
CORN FLAKES
Sprint
24
DU PONT
AUTOMOTIVE FINISHES
PENNZOIL

Burning Rubber

Can you spot . . .

- a letter J?
- a pliers?
- a red ribbon?
- a piano?
- a slice of pizza?
- a wire whisk?

Emergency, Emergency!

Can you spot . . .

- a chocolate sundae?
- a nurse's hat?
- a pink skirt?
- three dogs?
- a cup of tea?
- four bandage strips?

MERGENCY
MBULANCE
2002
AMBULANCE
FIRST
AID
AMBULANCE
Safety and Service
HIGHWAY PATROL
BANDAGES
AMBULANCE
CAUTION

Kickin' Up Dust

Can you spot . . .

- a grasshopper?
- an orange?
- a paw print?
- a frog?
- a dollar sign?
- a red bead?

Maisto

MBX
COAST PATROL
CARGO
CARGO
NASA
NASA
UNITED STATES OF AMERICA

Let's Jet

Can you spot . . .

- a mustache?
- a Lego?
- a tugboat?
- a ghost?
- a sign for women?
- two bats?

School Bus Rush

Can you spot . . .

- a teddy bear?
- a golden crown?
- a pumpkin?
- a fork?
- four striped bees?
- a spare tire?

TAXI
SCHOOL BUS
SCHOOL BUS
YIELD
YIELD
STOP
SCHOOL BUS
SCHOOL BUS
SCHOOL BUS
STOP
STOP
DARK TANNING OIL

G.I. Spy
Can you spot . . .
a clock?
a nest of eggs?
a camel?
a wrench?
a tarantula?
a toy train?

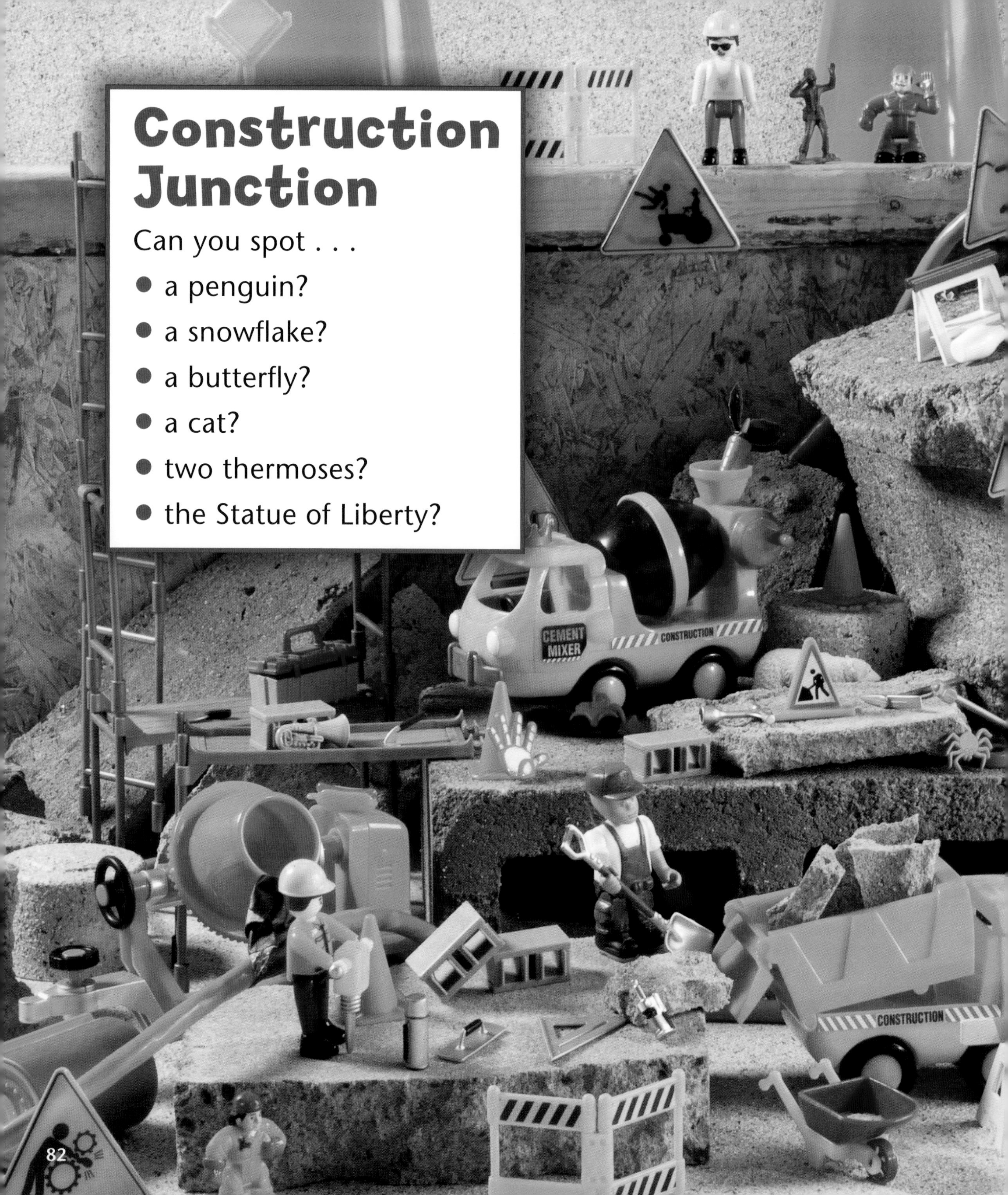

Construction Junction

Can you spot . . .

- a penguin?
- a snowflake?
- a butterfly?
- a cat?
- two thermoses?
- the Statue of Liberty?

STOP
CONSTRUCTION
TOWER CRANE
CAUTION

Out of This World!

Can you spot . . .

- an igloo?
- a bathtub?
- a milk jug?
- a jingle bell?
- three raccoons?
- a thimble?

AHEAD 6 MILES
KENNEDY
SPACE CENTER
OPEN 9:00AM TO 8:30PM
BUS TOURS 9:30 TO

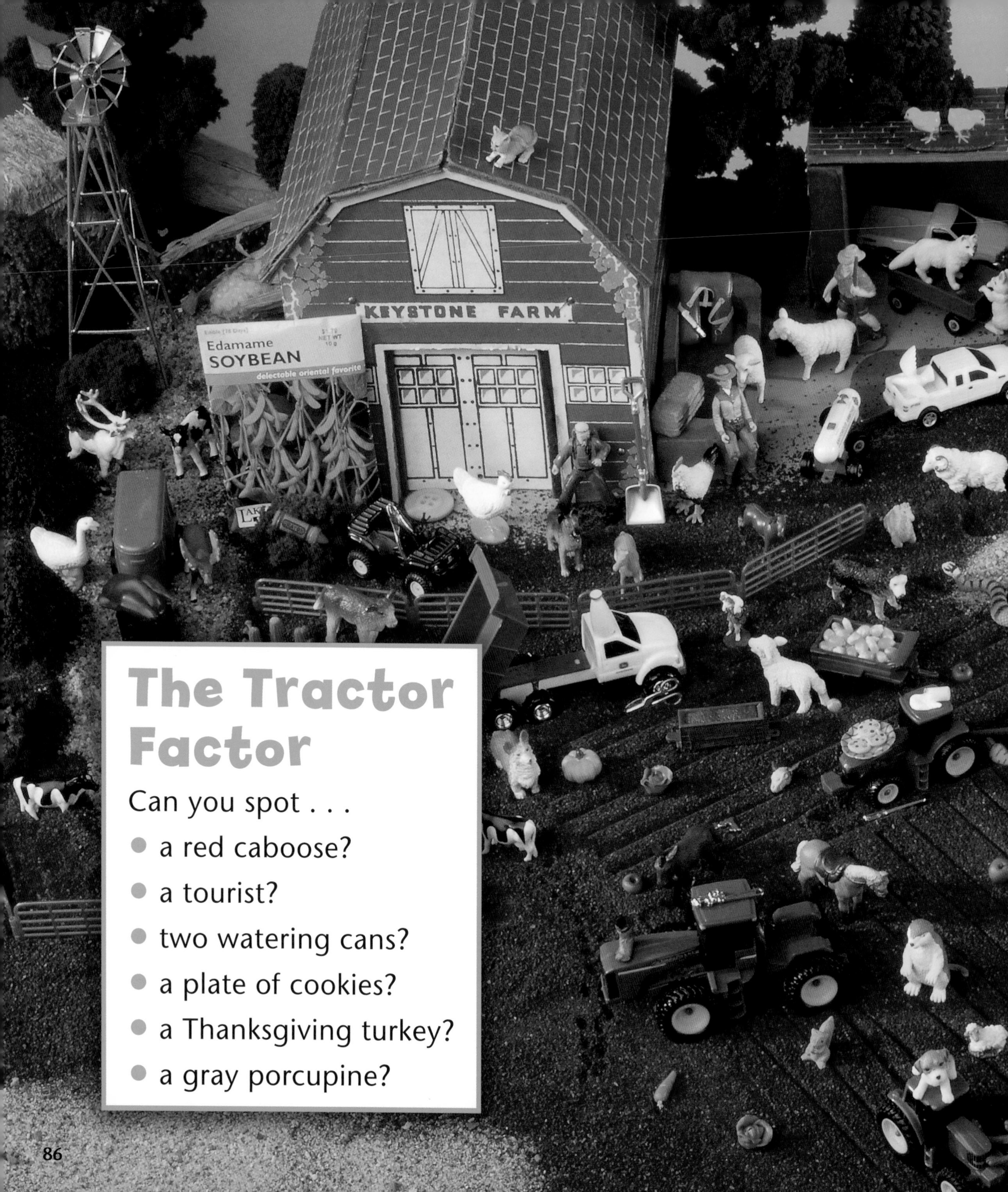

The Tractor Factor

Can you spot . . .

- a red caboose?
- a tourist?
- two watering cans?
- a plate of cookies?
- a Thanksgiving turkey?
- a gray porcupine?

Luffa Sponge
GOURD
$1.79
NET WT
2.5 g
easy and fun to grow
Cucuzzi
SQUASH
Italian heirloom variety
$1.79
NET WT
7 g

CHIEF

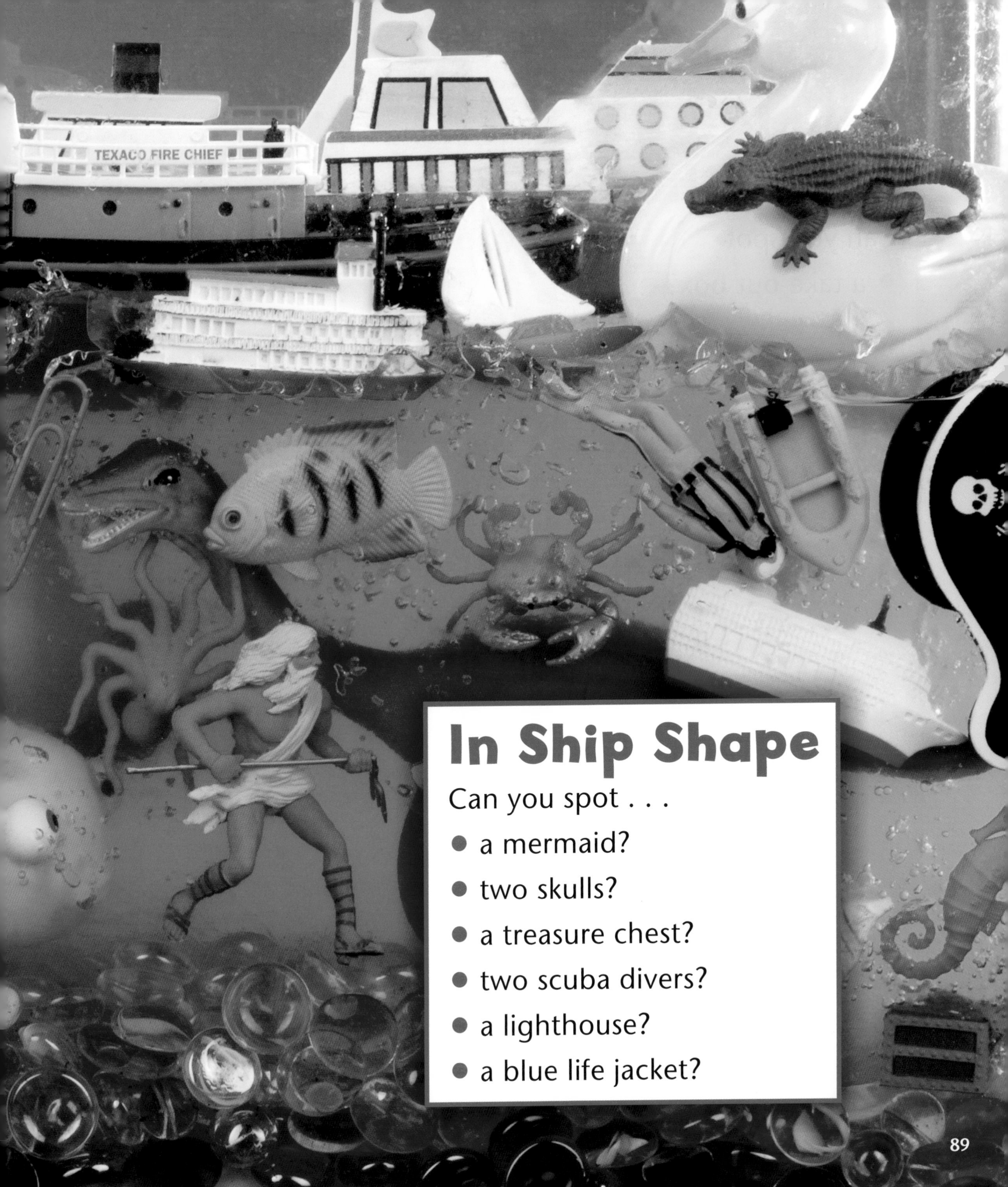

In Ship Shape

Can you spot . . .

- a mermaid?
- two skulls?
- a treasure chest?
- two scuba divers?
- a lighthouse?
- a blue life jacket?

Can I Get a Choo-Choo?

Can you spot . . .

- a take-out box?
- a picket fence?
- a high-fiving hand?
- five astronauts?
- a five-gallon pail?
- a pair of red shoes?

ONE WAY
POLICE
638
CHATTANOOGA
EMERGENCY
e can
dle it.
Be Specific—
ship UNION PACIFIC
BURLINGTON
NORTHERN
BN
100 024
689

inch
7-pc. Nut Driver Set
Made in U.S.A.
94196

From the Block

Can you spot . . .

- a camera?
- a battery?
- a trash can?
- an old TV?
- a clock?
- a toaster?

Spot Even More!

70 Burning Rubber

Try to find a clover, a safety pin, a flower, a hatchet, a hammer, a saxophone, a hot dog, and a sea star.

72 Emergency, Emergency!

See if you can spot a pair of rubber boots, a red button, two fire extinguishers, and a thermometer.

74 Kickin' Up Dust

Take another look and find a green spider, a palm tree, a red car, a saddle, a football helmet, and a heart.

76 Let's Jet

Now find a pirate ship, an eraser, a hot air balloon, a spell book, a toucan, a letter L, and an oar.

78 School Bus Rush

Now spot a dump truck, a bottle of tanning oil, a yellow crayon, a shining sun, and a fish.

80 G.I. Spy

Try to spy a crocodile, a football, a gingerbread man, a cowboy hat, army dog tags, and a teddy bear.

82 Construction Junction

See if you can spy a spider web, a gray horn, a carrot, a horseshoe, two shovels, and an orange car.

84 Out of This World!

Try to find an elephant, a white shoe, a black shoe, a glittery moon, and eleven American flags.

86 The Tractor Factor

Now spot a bone, a sea star, some cow tracks, an orange button, a life jacket, a coffeepot, and three planes.

88 In Ship Shape

Try to find two blue eyes, two toothy mouths, a pair of sandals, a red flag, and three pincers.

90 Can I Get a Choo-Choo?

Now look for a rooster, a top hat, an arctic fox, a monster truck, green sunglasses, and two soldiers.

92 From the Block

Take one last look to find a white thumbtack, a gold jack, two cookie cutters, a motorcycle, and a silver car.

DO NOT ENTER
USA
PARKING
U.S. COAST GUARD
STOP
SCHOOL BUS
MEDICAL SERVICES
EMERGENCY
AMBULANCE
WRONG WAY
SCHOOL BUS

Extreme Spot-It Challenge

Just can't get enough Spot-It action? Try this extra challenge. See if you can spot:

- **a blue convertible**
- **two stop signs**
- **a tree**
- **a key**
- **a safari jeep**
- **a bumblebee**
- **a blimp**
- **a Jet Ski**
- **a white convertible**
- **a blue van**
- **a saw**
- **a spare tire**
- **a bowling pin**
- **a red barn**
- **an anchor**
- **a covered wagon**
- **a moon rover**

CHRISTMAS FUN

CRAYON

Snow Folk Gathering

Can you spot . . .

- a woodland gnome?
- a green fish?
- a bumblebee?
- a button cap?
- a bathroom sink?
- a broom?

A Doggone Christmas

Can you spot . . .

- a naughty squirrel?
- a basket of yarn?
- a cowboy boot?
- a pliers?
- a wire whisk?
- a red teacup?

FIRS
AID
MILK
S

X-Mess Decorations
Can you spot . . .
• a rubber chicken?
• a toilet seat?
• a cement mixer?
• a wooden train?
• a real hot dog?
• a faceless friend?
• a yellow wrench?
Mini SUDOKU

Gift Wrap Madness

Can you spot . . .

- a bone?
- a blue watch?
- a baseball?
- a bowling pin?
- a pencil sharpener?
- a pair of binoculars?

Scotch
GILL
JUMBO ROLL
YoYo
8
KISS
LOVE

Ding-a-Ling, Bells Ring

Can you spot . . .

- a silver car?
- two tiny trumpets?
- a nickel?
- a musical tie?
- a fishing hook?
- a slinky?
- an eraser?
- a fire chief's badge?

Angels
We Have Heard
On High
Sleighride Fantasy
To Elizabeth Anna Dawson
Joy to the World

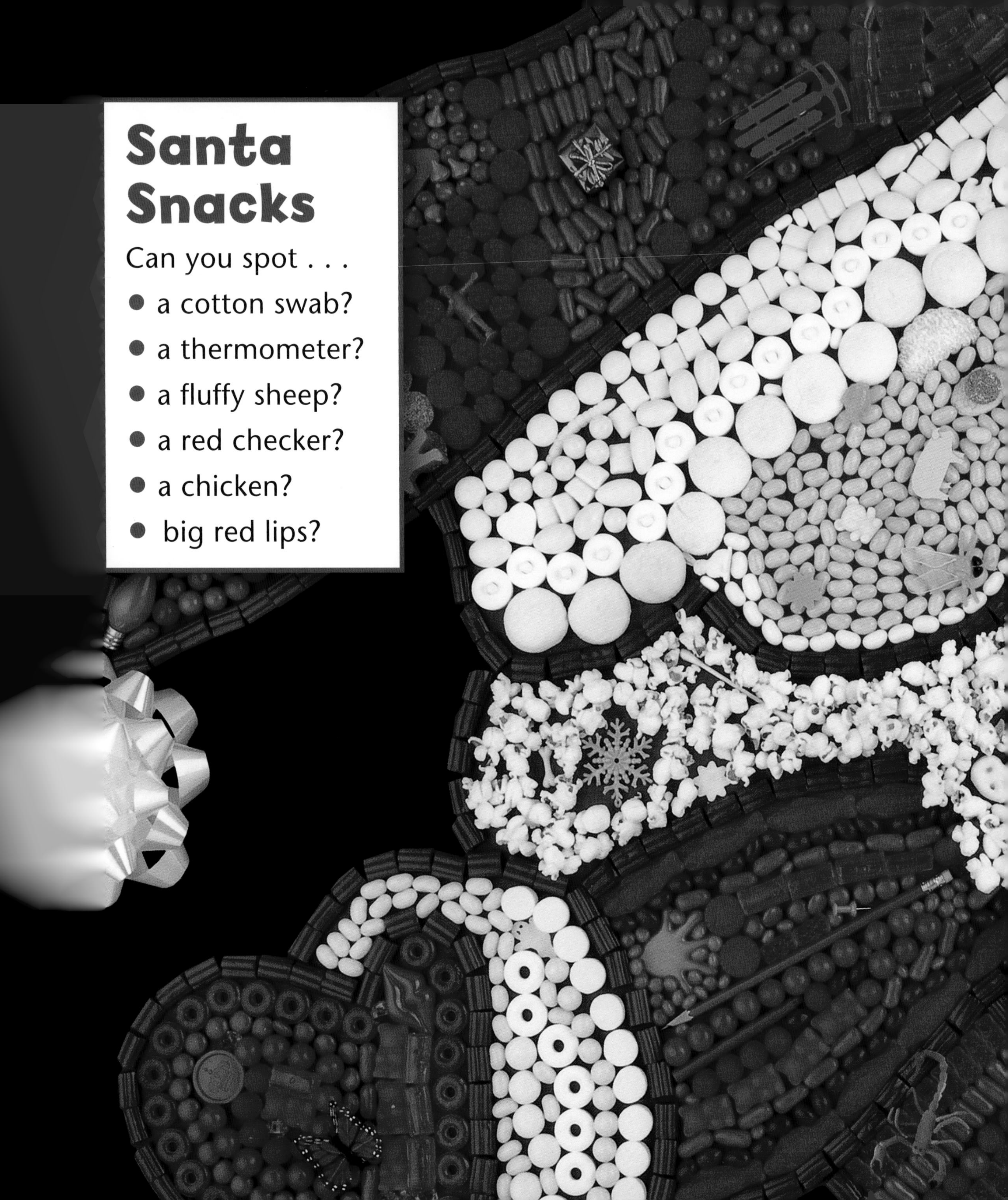

Santa Snacks

Can you spot . . .

- a cotton swab?
- a thermometer?
- a fluffy sheep?
- a red checker?
- a chicken?
- big red lips?

USA

Merry Christmas

A Tropical Christmas

Can you spot . . .

- Santa Claus?
- an eye patch?
- a fire hydrant?
- a paddle?
- a treasure chest?
- a sailboat?
- a tiny angel?

Beastly Christmas Feast

Can you spot . . .

- a pink flamingo?
- a ketchup bottle?
- two artichokes?
- a red bathtub?
- a fire truck?
- a red mushroom?
- a number 1?

KISS ME
#1 FAN

Tickets
BUS
STOP

Gingerbread Village
Can you spot . . .
• four lost mittens?
• a camel?
• a cowboy?
• a globe?
• a snorkel?
• a headless horseman?
• a pinecone?

ABCDEFGHIJKLM NOPQRSTUVWXYZ
12345 67890
Fun to Play HARMONICA
jaymar
At Your Service! BELL

ILLINOIS TERMINAL
Bears in a Boat
CHECKER

Dominoes
FARM ABC

Toys for Christmas

Can you spot . . .

- a seashell?
- a fork?
- an apple?
- a merry-go-round?
- a blue letter J?
- an ice cream scoop?

Blue, Blue Christmas

Can you spot . . .

- a spotted toad?
- a paper clip?
- some cool shades?
- two elephants?
- a football helmet?
- a toothbrush?
- a dinosaur?

D
S
JOY

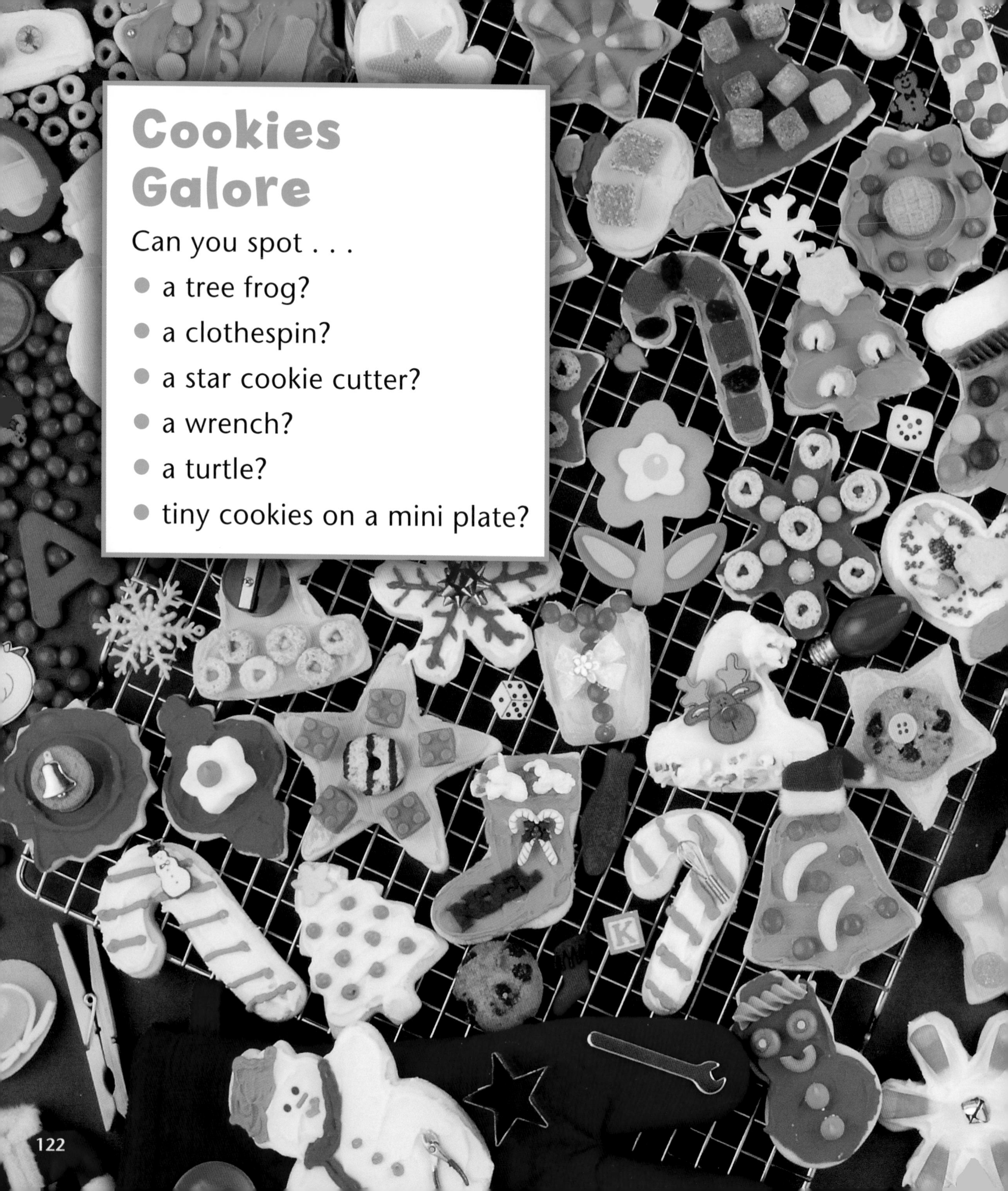

Cookies Galore

Can you spot . . .

- a tree frog?
- a clothespin?
- a star cookie cutter?
- a wrench?
- a turtle?
- tiny cookies on a mini plate?

M

Spot Even More!

Snow Folk Gathering

Try to find a hiker, a fire hydrant, a toilet, a cone, a tiny rake, a green paper clip, and a piece of candy corn.

A Doggone Christmas

Try to spot a cake, a mouse, a carrot, a mousetrap, a hot dog, a leaf, and a big shoe.

X-Mess Decorations

Take another look and find an airplane, a soldier, a ship, a sandwich, a blue house fly, and a fishing fish.

Gift Wrap Madness

Now find a ladybug, a shiny pickle, fuzzy dice, a sea horse, two dinosaurs, and a winner's trophy.

Ding-a-Ling, Bells Ring

Now spot a strawberry, five Christmas stockings, a nail clipper, and two bell-shaped cookie cutters.

Santa Snacks

Try to spy some glasses, a dove, a number 1 fan hand, a sled, a scorpion, an egg, and a jeep.

112

A Tropical Christmas

See if you can find a skeleton, red Christmas bells, an octopus, a chair, and a pair of earmuffs.

114

Beastly Christmas Feast

Try to find a cowboy hat, a butterfly, a mitten, a roll of toilet paper, white shoelaces, and a soccer ball.

116

Gingerbread Village

Now spot a gumball machine, a green monster, a bunny with a carrot, a teddy bear, and Santa Claus.

118

Toys for Christmas

Try to find a green colored pencil, an airplane, a sheriff's star, a banana, and a sand castle.

120

Blue, Blue Christmas

Now look for a tiny blue car, two silver stars, a sea horse, a sparkly white pear, and two butterflies.

122

Cookies Galore

Take one last look and find a red "A," a yellow button, a comb, Santa's boots, a pink shoe, and a silver bell.

Tickets

Extreme Spot-It Challenge

Just can't get enough Spot-It action? Find the items in this extra Christmas challenge.

- **ticket booth**
- **taxi**
- **officer's badge**
- **spoon**
- **the ace of spades**
- **skateboard**
- **black shoe**
- **penny**
- **white dove**
- **two blue trees**
- **drinking straw**
- **two gingerbread cookie cutters**
- **ear of corn**
- **battery**
- **bar of soap**
- **green snake**
- **wooden match**